199
REASONS
TO BE
THANKFUL

199 REASONS TO BE THANKFUL

Janice Hanna

BARBOUR
PUBLISHING

To my children and grandchildren. I'm so thankful for all of you.

Published by Barbour Publishing, Inc., P.O. Box 719, Uhrichsville, Ohio 44683, www.barbourbooks.com

Our mission is to publish and distribute inspirational products offering exceptional value and biblical encouragement to the masses.

Member of the
Evangelical Christian
Publishers Association

Printed in the United States of America.

1

OUR HEAVENLY FATHER

We have a Father in heaven who adores us. Unlike our earthly father, the Lord's love for us is unconditional. This wonderful, awesome Daddy God is the Creator of the universe. That means He's the maker and manufacturer of everything. . .including you.

Because you are sons, God sent the Spirit of his Son into our hearts, the Spirit who calls out, "Abba, Father."
GALATIANS 4:6 NIV

2

JESUS, GOD'S ONLY SON

Jesus Christ—fully God, fully man. Our way to the Father. How can we ever begin to thank Him for leaving heaven to walk among us? We are saved by His blood, healed by His stripes, and delivered by His sacrifice. There is none like Him. He alone came to save us from our sins. And one day every knee will bow and every tongue confess that Jesus Christ is Lord!

Jesus, when I think about the great sacrifice You made,
leaving heaven and coming to earth. . .for me. . .
I'm overwhelmed. Thank You for Your sacrifice on
the cross and for offering Yourself for my sins. Amen.

3

THE HOLY SPIRIT, OUR COMFORTER

We have a Comforter, One who fully understands our deepest longings and pains, One who embraces us when we need it most. That's why Jesus told His followers to be on the lookout for the very best Comforter of all. The Holy Spirit wraps us in His arms and breathes peace into our tired souls.

Lord, thank You for sending a Comforter!
There are so many times I don't know where
I'd be if I didn't feel the comforting embrace
of the Spirit of God. Amen.

4

GOD'S GLORIOUS CREATION

Can you imagine what it must have been like to view God's glorious creation at the end of that very first week? Majestic mountaintops. Rushing rivers. The lush, green garden. What a creative and loving God we serve!

And God saw every thing that he had made, and, behold, it was very good. And the evening and the morning were the sixth day.

GENESIS 1:31 KJV

5

SABBATH REST

In this crazy workaholic world we live in, rest is tough to come by. We run full steam ahead all day long and then struggle to sleep when we finally tumble into bed. God ordained rest. It's one of His greatest gifts to us, and one we should be very thankful for!

6

GODLY DISCERNMENT

Have you praised Him for the many times He has guided and directed you. . .kept you from making wrong decisions? Discernment is truly a gift, one that helps us make godly choices every step of the way.

7
GOD'S GRACE

Because Jesus was willing to lay down His life to pay for our sins, we not only gain entrance into heaven, we share in all heavenly riches. Grace is something we didn't earn, and it's something we can't lose. It's a gift, one that is poured out on us, especially when we don't deserve it. Aren't you thankful for this marvelous gift?

But by the grace of God I am what I am,
and his grace to me was not without effect. No,
I worked harder than all of them—yet not I,
but the grace of God that was with me.

1 CORINTHIANS 15:10 NIV

8

THE WORD OF GOD

The Bible is so accessible! For hundreds of years, churchgoers were kept away from this amazing book—God's "owner's manual" for His children. Now, twenty-first–century believers are just a click away on the World Wide Web. What a blessing!

For the word of God is quick, and powerful,
and sharper than any twoedged sword, piercing even to
the dividing asunder of soul and spirit, and of
the joints and marrow, and is a discerner of
the thoughts and intents of the heart.

HEBREWS 4:12 KJV

9

A FAVORITE PET

A pet can comfort you when you're down; he will never judge you and will love you unconditionally, regardless of any mistakes you might have made. How good of God, to create these creatures for our enjoyment. They are such a gift.

Lord, it might seem a little silly to thank You for my pet, but I'm so grateful to have a companion who loves me unconditionally. It's such a great reminder that Your love is greater still. . .even when I make mistakes. Amen.

10

SILENCE

S ilence is a gift, especially in this loud, crazy world we live in. Too often, instead of being thankful for it, we dread it. We fill every minute of the day with noise—music, conversation, television, video games—all in an attempt to drown out the quiet. Make some time to enjoy God's gift of silence.

A time to rend, and a time to sew;
a time to keep silence, and a time to speak.

ECCLESIASTES 3:7 KJV

11
MY LOCAL CHURCH

It's a wonderful thing to be part of something. It's even more wonderful when that "something" is the body of Christ. When you find a place that fits—a place where your gifts and talents can be utilized—you can flourish.

12
EMPLOYMENT

God is our Jehovah-jireh, our provider. He cares for our every need, including the job we work. Maybe you're in a job that you love. Perhaps you're still looking for that "dream job." Regardless of your situation, spend some time thanking the Lord for being your provider!

13

FAMILY

Our parents, siblings, children, grandparents, aunts, uncles, and cousins are all packages to be unwrapped and treasured. Oh, they might not be perfect (who among us is?) but they're quirky, fun, and offbeat—we complement each other like pieces of a puzzle—and that more than makes up for a lack of perfection.

Dear Lord, may I never forget to thank
You for my family. They are Your gift to me.
I know our family will never be perfect,
but I'm thankful for each of them. Amen.

14

Jesus' work on
the cross

In one sacrificial act, Jesus offered Himself
as atonement for all. Oh, the blood of Jesus!
It truly washes me whiter than snow. May we
never take the work of the cross for granted.

Together as one body, Christ reconciled both groups
to God by means of his death on the cross, and our
hostility toward each other was put to death.

EPHESIANS 2:16 NLT

A THIRST-QUENCHING DRINK OF WATER

For a parched throat, there's nothing more satisfying than a long dreg of crystal-clear ice water. We may try to quench our thirst with other liquids—tea, soft drinks, juice—but authentic, life-sustaining water is the only drink that remedies the deep dryness of thirst.

Jesus answered, "Everyone who drinks this water will be thirsty again, but whoever drinks the water I give him will never thirst. Indeed, the water I give him will become in him a spring of water welling up to eternal life."

JOHN 4:13—14 NIV

16

A GOOD EDUCATION

An education opens doors of opportunity throughout a lifetime. Maybe you or your parents had to make sacrifices for you to get a good education. Praise God for the path He provided for this blessing on your life.

A wise man will hear, and will increase learning; and a man of understanding shall attain unto wise counsels.

PROVERBS 1:5 KJV

THE SCENT OF A NEWBORN, FRESH FROM GOD

Have you ever held a newborn baby and looked into his precious face? Smelled the scent of baby lotion on her skin? What a wondrous thing. . .the innocence of a child new to this earth. Each new life is a reminder from above of the Lord's overwhelming love for His children.

Like newborn babies, you must crave pure spiritual milk so that you will grow into a full experience of salvation. Cry out for this nourishment.

1 PETER 2:2 NLT

18

EVERY KNEE WILL BOW AND EVERY TONGUE CONFESS

Does it amaze you to think that people from every tribe and nation will one day acknowledge the fact that Jesus is God's Son, the Savior of the world? Can you imagine what that chorus of voices will sound like? Oh, praise God for that day!

At the name of Jesus every knee should bow,
in heaven and on earth and under the earth.

PHILIPPIANS 2:10 NIV

19

NEW BEGINNINGS

Every time you get a fresh start, a chance to begin again, Jesus is right there at the center of it. His forgiveness empowers us to look ahead, not back.

20

THE SOUND OF THE OCEAN

The sound of ocean waves lapping the shoreline is a reminder of the power and presence of an all-knowing God. And they're also a reminder that life moves in ebbs and flows. . .the problems that rush in today, flow out tomorrow.

21

UNEXPECTED SURPRISES

God loves to bless His kids with unexpected surprises. When they happen, it's as if the Lord has leaned down to whisper, "I'm still here! I care!"

Lord, thanks for the many, many times You've moved unexpectedly in my life. Those surprises have warmed my heart and reminded me that You're interested in the everyday things of my life. Amen.

22

GOD'S HOLY PRESENCE

You can never go too far from God's Spirit, and you can't flee from His presence. Now that's something to be thankful for. The Lord wants you to come to Him—for forgiveness of sins, for times of intimacy with Him, and to offer up your cares and concerns. He issues an invitation daily for you to enjoy His holy presence.

I can never escape from your Spirit!
I can never get away from your presence!

PSALM 139:7 NLT

23
UNCONDITIONAL LOVE

His unconditional love reaches out to us, even when we don't deserve it...especially when we don't deserve it. Oh, that we could learn to love one another unconditionally!

24
GODLY TEACHERS

Godly teachers train us to follow after the Lord wholeheartedly. By their example, we're taught how to grow into the men and women of God we're called to be. Thank God for every single one who's had an impact on you!

25

CORPORATE WORSHIP

One day we'll gather around the throne of God singing, "Holy, holy, holy is the Lord God Almighty, who was and is and is to come!" Till then, we sing the songs He's laid on the hearts of men, songs of praise and worship. Thank Him for the opportunity to come together in one accord with other believers to worship.

Let us come before him with thanksgiving
and extol him with music and song.

PSALM 95:2 NIV

26

GOD'S ABILITY TO MULTIPLY
MY LOAVES AND FISHES

We serve a miracle-working God. He has the ability to take what little we give Him—our time, talents, and treasures—and multiply them! What do you have today? Just a mustard seed of faith? Give it to Him and watch how He multiplies it!

Jesus took the five loaves and two fish, looked up toward heaven, and blessed them. Then, breaking the loaves into pieces, he kept giving the bread and fish to the disciples so they could distribute it to the people.

LUKE 9:16 NLT

27

GOD'S HAND OF BLESSING

What does it mean to be blessed? To the world, that means health, wealth, and happiness. Jesus says that we're blessed beyond measure even when things don't seem to be going our way. Truth is, God's blessings encompass us with every good thing—tangible and intangible—all because He loves us!

28

MEDICAL KNOW-HOW

How wonderful that we live in such a technologically advanced age, where medical research is going on around us. Thank God for modern medicine!

MODERN CONVENIENCES

Fifty years ago, there were no personal computers, no Internet, no cell phones, no ATM machines, no microwaves. We didn't use debit cards, and we couldn't watch televised images from the other side of the world in real time. This twenty-first-century world we live in is amazing! We have so much to be thankful for.

Lord, I'm thankful for modern conveniences. Sometimes I take them for granted, but I'm so grateful for the blessings they bring to my life. Amen.

30

QUIET TIME WITH GOD

When we slip away to a quiet place—a time with our Father God—we're reminded of His love, His grace, His mercy. We lean our head against His chest and call out to Him then listen as He whispers His Words of love to our souls. Where would we be without this special time with our heavenly Father?

You will seek me and find me when
you seek me with all your heart.

JEREMIAH 29:13 NIV

31
DO-OVERS

Do you ever wish you could go back and start the day over? Have a second chance? Praise God. . .the Christian life is full of do-overs! Our forgiving God gives us second, third, and fourth chances!

32
LAUGHTER THAT
BUBBLES UP

Laughter rises up from a joyful heart! God placed it there as an outward expression of innermost joy. Now that's something to be thankful for!

33

PATIENCE

Patience is one of those character attributes that everyone needs, but few of us have. Without God's help, we're tapping our toes, checking our watches, and getting frustrated by the minute. Ask God to infuse your personality with patience when you need it, and then give the glory to Him.

The end of a thing is better than its beginning;
The patient in spirit is better than the proud in spirit.

ECCLESIASTES 7:8 NKJV

34

SILLY E-MAILS

Silly e-mails often come at just the right time, when you're frustrated or needing a lift. The next time you get one in your inbox, don't delete it! Instead, read it and have a good, long laugh. It'll do your heart good!

A merry heart doeth good like a medicine:
but a broken spirit drieth the bones.

PROVERBS 17:22 KJV

35
HANDMADE QUILTS

Take a close look at all of the colors of a handmade quilt. Examine the intricate stitches. In some ways, the body of Christ is like a quilt, lovingly stitched by the Lord. May we, like that quilt, be a thing of beauty to a watching world.

36
THE 20-ITEMS-OR-LESS AISLE

With just a handful of items in your basket, you're convinced you'll have to wait forever to check out. Then you see it! The 20-items-or-less aisle. A shortcut! In that moment, it almost seems. . .miraculous!

THE CLOSENESS OF GOD

God is as near as a whispered prayer, as close as your very breath. And He longs for you to draw near to Him on a regular basis. And when you're going through a rough time, He wants you to share your burdens with Him in prayer.

*Before a word is on my tongue
you know it completely, O LORD.*

PSALM 139:4 NIV

38
CONSTELLATIONS

Do the twinkling stars stir up your imagination, making you think you could reach out and pluck one from the sky? Imagine what fun God had creating the constellations—spinning them off into space and then holding them there to bring us light.

I consider your heavens, the work of your fingers, the moon and the stars, which you have set in place.

PSALM 8:3 NIV

39

A SENSE OF HUMOR

A sense of humor is a lifesaver when things around us are spiraling out of control. Take time to laugh. . .and to thank the One who gave you the gift of humor in the first place. A little goes a long, long way!

40

AN UNEXPECTED NOTE FROM A FRIEND

It's so nice to get a great note from a friend . . .even better when it arrives on a day you're needing encouragement. God has written the greatest note of all, His Word. When you're looking for a pick-me-up, read what He's got to say about how much He loves you!

41

REALIZING I HAVE NOTHING TO WORRY ABOUT

What a relief to know we can hand our troubles over to the King of Kings. We don't have to fret! God is calling you to a worry-free life. This might seem impossible, but the Lord is certainly capable of handling our concerns. Best of all, He offers to lift those worries right out of our hands.

Therefore do not worry about tomorrow,
for tomorrow will worry about itself.
Each day has enough trouble of its own.

MATTHEW 6:34 NIV

42

FRESH AIR

Lungs full of fresh air are something we take for granted until we're stuck in the recycled air of an airplane or in the middle of a smog-laden city. Take a deep breath and appreciate the life-giving refreshment of fresh air.

Then the LORD God formed the man from the dust of the ground. He breathed the breath of life into the man's nostrils, and the man became a living person.

GENESIS 2:7 NLT

43
THE FIRST CHRISTMAS LIGHTS OF THE SEASON

As you see tiny lights twinkle against the evening sky, be reminded of that night so long ago when a star shone over Bethlehem, lighting the birth of the eternal King.

44
LONG, LEISURELY WALKS

Sidewalks, cornfields, park pathways, and winding country roads all invite us to take long, leisurely walks. These treks are perfect for reconnecting with a spouse, friend, pet, and even God.

45

RAINBOWS

Rainbows bring hope. They remind us of God's promise to Noah and His promise of a hopeful future to us, His children. They also serve as a reminder that the storms of life won't last forever. There's a brighter tomorrow coming if we can just hold onto the hand of the Creator of the rainbow.

And God said unto Noah, This is the token of the covenant, which I have established between me and all flesh that is upon the earth.

GENESIS 9:17 KJV

I AM UNIQUELY AND WONDERFULLY MADE

It's so easy to look at the reflection in the mirror and see the flaws. Instead we should look in the mirror and marvel at how God took the time to create us—as individuals. No more grumbling over the color of your eyes or the length of your nose! Instead, thank Him for making you unique!

I will praise You, for I am fearfully and wonderfully made; marvelous are Your works, and that my soul knows very well.

PSALM 139:14 NKJV

47

RAIN AFTER A DRY SPELL

Ah, the refreshment of drought-ending rain. The thirsty earth begs for water so that it can be replenished, restored. And a weary heart cries out for spiritual water, so that it can keep going.

48

FREEDOM

We have freedom all around us: freedom to worship; freedom to witness to others without fear; freedom from our past sins—the list is endless. We are a blessed people!

49
MY HEALTH

If you've ever been through a serious illness, then you know just how fragile life can be. It's difficult to understand why we get sick or why everyone isn't healed. But one thing is very clear: Each day we experience health is a precious gift.

Lord, how do I begin to thank You for the gift of health?
Thank You for the many times You've healed me, and
thank You for walking me through the tough times.
I'm so grateful for Your health plan! Amen.

50
CRITIQUE

Receiving helpful criticism from others can help develop and grow us into the people of God we're called to be. How well we handle critique is up to us. Instead of grumbling when people offer their suggestions and comments, begin to praise the Lord.

Lord, I'll admit it's not always easy to accept criticism. I cringe when some of those things are spoken over me, especially the hard things. Help me to be thankful for every critique—the ones that are easy to hear. . . and the ones that are difficult. Amen.

51
ELECTRICITY

Where would we be without electricity? As you flip that switch, pause for a moment to thank God for this tool that makes our lives so much easier.

52
THE SMELL OF COFFEE IN THE MORNING

Coffee works like a magnet, drawing you from your slumber to face the tasks of the day. It energizes and invigorates. As you grab that first cup, may it serve as a reminder to spend some quiet time in your Bible and in prayer.

53
CHANGING SEASONS

Oh, seasons! Feeling the cold chill of winter lift. Watching that first flower burst through the spring sod. Hearing children at play in the summer. Seeing the leaves morph to red, gold, and brown in the fall. Nature's seasons are perfectly timed, and so are the personal seasons you go through. Aren't you thankful the hard times don't last forever? God knew what He was doing when He designed them to come . . .and go.

There is a time for everything, and a
season for every activity under heaven.

ECCLESIASTES 3:1 NIV

54

HEALTHY CHILDREN

If your children—young or old—are walking in health, what a blessing! If any of them are struggling with health issues, remember to praise God through the storms. He loves your children even more than you do, after all!

Lord, thank You for healthy children.
Forgive me for not mentioning this more often.
Sometimes I forget to thank You.
And for those who are struggling with their health. . .
Father, today I ask for healing for every unhealthy child.
Amen.

55

GRANDPA'S WHISKERY KISS

Perhaps you have a grandmother or grandfather who poured themselves into your life, who let you know you were loved, who encouraged you with kisses. What treasured memories! What a blessing!

56

A LOVING SPOUSE

A spouse who loves you and loves the Lord is a gift from on high. There is something so special about the love between husband and wife, especially when they're walking in unity. Talk about the perfect picture of Christ and the church!

57

GOD STILL LOVES ME
DESPITE MYSELF

Doesn't it do your heart good to remember that God loves you. . .in spite of yourself? There's nothing you can do to cause God to stop loving you. Oh, aren't you thankful for His unconditional love?

Nor height, nor depth, nor any other creature, shall be able to separate us from the love of God, which is in Christ Jesus our Lord.

ROMANS 8:39 KJV

CHILDREN WHO LOVE THE LORD

You can watch them in church, singing at the top of their lungs. You can see them in Sunday school class, hungry to know more about God. You can watch them at home, sharing toys and speaking words of love over their brothers and sisters. Oh, the beauty of a child who truly, wholeheartedly loves God.

Train a child in the way he should go,
and when he is old he will not turn from it.

PROVERBS 22:6 NIV

59
LAUNDRY

Piles of laundry are proof of God's provision for us—we have clothes to wear! Next time you stare at a pile of dirty shirts, pants, socks, and underwear, whisper a prayer of thanks that God provides for your needs.

60
A PRODUCTIVE DAY

There's no better feeling than crossing off tasks on a lengthy to-do list. Some days we find ourselves in super-productive mode and can cross off more than we normally do. Celebrate those days as a job *very* well done!

61

ROAD MAPS

Road maps offer us guidance in the unfamiliar areas we travel. God has a road map for our lives, too. The Bible—His Word— is our ultimate map. Today, take the time to thank God for guidance and direction, both physical and spiritual!

Lord, I thank You for Your direction in my life.
You've been there every step of the way, guiding me.
Keep me on the narrow road, Father. May
every step be in Your direction. Amen.

UNEXPECTED ENCOURAGEMENT

A bad morning can turn into a bad day that turns into a bad week. But sometimes all it takes is an unexpected kind word from a coworker, a spouse, or a friend, to turn a bad time into a joy-filled day. Thank God for these surprise blessings and ask Him to show you opportunities to be the giver of some unexpected encouragement.

Encourage one another and build each other up, just as in fact you are doing.

1 THESSALONIANS 5:11 NIV

63
GOD'S ECONOMICS

God's got all financial matters under control. When it looks as if your dollar won't stretch to cover your month, the Lord knows just what to do. All you have to do is ask.

64
SUPPORTIVE FRIENDS

Godly friends are a great support system. They lift your arms when you're weary and encourage you to keep going when you feel like giving up. Isn't it wonderful to see how God strategically placed the ones you needed in just the right place at just the right time?

65
FREEDOM TO WORSHIP

There are so many places around the globe where worship is illegal, forcing believers to take their celebrations underground. What a blessing it is to be able to worship when and where we want! Thank God for this freedom, and while you're at it, pray for those who aren't allowed to worship freely.

For you have been called to live in freedom, my brothers and sisters. But don't use your freedom to satisfy your sinful nature. Instead, use your freedom to serve one another in love.

GALATIANS 5:13 NLT

66

FORGIVENESS

When God offers us forgiveness of sins, He's releasing us from our guilt and shame, too. And what He freely offers us, He expects us to offer others as well. So, if you're holding someone in unforgiveness today, open those hands and let it go. Forgive. . .as you've been forgiven.

Lord, I can't thank You enough for Your forgiveness.
All of my sins. . .washed away!
It seems impossible, and yet it's true.
Now, Father, may I be just as forgiving
of others when they hurt me.
Thank You for the gift of forgiveness. Amen.

67

A PLACE TO PILLOW MY HEAD

Ah, sleep! Curling up in bed after a long, tiring day, closing our eyes. . .and drifting away to slumber-land. Take the time to thank God that He's given you a place to lay your head at night. Oh, that glorious bed, that cushy, comfy gift from on high!

68

GREAT FOOD

What do you enjoy most? Pasta? Fajitas? Steak and baked potato? Yum! It all sounds good, right? We're so blessed to have access to so many great foods. Today, take the time to really thank God for the provision of your "daily bread."

69

FINANCIAL PROVISION

We serve a "just enough and just in time" God, don't we? He manages to prove Himself in the area of financial provision time and time again. And aren't you even more thankful for His many blessings during the "lean" times?

Give, and it will be given to you: good measure, pressed down, shaken together, and running over will be put into your bosom. For with the same measure that you use, it will be measured back to you.

LUKE 6:38 NKJV

— 70 —
HEARTFELT APOLOGIES

Fences can be mended in a moment as those life-changing words, "I'm sorry, I was wrong. Will you forgive me?" are spoken. Do you need to apologize to someone today? Maybe you need to accept someone's apology. Regardless, today is your day!

Lord, thank You for giving me the courage to apologize when I need to. It's not always easy, but it's so freeing! And thank You for giving me the courage to forgive others when they've hurt me. . .whether they ever apologize or not. Amen.

71
DEWY MORNINGS

A dewy morning reminds us that each day is fresh—that you can forget about yesterday's worries. They were washed away in the night by that heavenly dew.

72
A LULLABY

Can you hear it now. . .a mother's loving voice singing over her children, easing that little one off to dreamland? Did you know that God sings over you? Just like a mother rejoices over her little one with singing, your heavenly Father croons His love song over you.

A WARM SHOWER AFTER A GRIMY DAY

Ah, that awesome feeling of washing away every bit of dirt. There's nothing to compare with being really, really clean after a dirty day of hard work. Somehow that water takes with it every bit of frustration, angst, and confusion. It dribbles down the drain, never to be seen again.

Wash me thoroughly from my iniquity,
and cleanse me from my sin.

PSALM 51:2 NKJV

74

PLANTING SEEDS AND WATCHING THEM GROW

What a fabulous moment. . .when you see that tiny shoot peek out of the ground. Then, day by day, you watch it become what it is meant to be. Something bigger. Something worthwhile.

Lord, thank You for designing the world in such a way that things grow. It's so fun to watch plants morph and change over time. And it's fun to watch the growth in my own life, too. Amen.

75

WRITTEN WORDS THAT
STIR MY SOUL

God has gifted Christian writers with both the desire and the talent to reach others with their words. Those who walk intimately with their Savior have fresh insight to share with readers. Thank God for books you've read. . .and the authors who penned them.

76

SUNDAY NAPS

There's no better time for a long, luxurious nap than on Sunday afternoon. There's something about resting on the Lord's Day that feels extra special. Rest in Him today.

77
MY HOME

Maybe the walls of your home need a fresh coat of paint or the roof needs replacing. Perhaps your furniture is outdated or worn. In the grand scheme of things, those things don't matter at all, do they? God has blessed you with a safe haven. A place to go, away from the troubles of the world. Now, that's definitely something to be thankful for.

Then the king said to the man of God, "Come home with me and refresh yourself, and I will give you a reward."

1 KINGS 13:7 NKJV

THE SOUND OF FAMILY OPENING CHRISTMAS PRESENTS

Pause a moment to think about all of the Christmases you have celebrated over the years—past and present. There's something rather magical about family gift exchanges. Perhaps it's the symbolic reminder of the many gifts our heavenly Father pours out on us, His children.

And when they were come into the house, they saw the young child with Mary his mother, and fell down, and worshipped him: and when they had opened their treasures, they presented unto him gifts; gold, and frankincense and myrrh.

MATTHEW 2:11 KJV

79
FRESH-BAKED COOKIES

Whether you're keen on peanut butter, chocolate chip, or oatmeal raisin cookies, there's something amazing about the scent of homemade cookies, fresh from the oven. Mmm. . .yummy!

80
ENTERTAINMENT

Whether it's dinner and a movie with your best friend or a game of skee-ball with the one you love, entertainment can be a nice distraction from life's cares.

81

GOD WILL MAKE A WAY

Have you ever faced a seemingly impossible situation, only to see the Lord move in a miraculous way? Were you amazed? We shouldn't be stunned when the Lord moves on our behalf. God is in the deliverance business! He will make a way when there seems to be no way. Now, that's something to be thankful for!

Lord, I'm thankful for the many times You've intervened in my life, making a way when I thought there was no way. You are truly the God of the impossible.

82

PLANES, TRAINS, AND AUTOMOBILES

A hundred years ago, most people still traveled by wagon or horseback. Those on longer journeys took the train. Today we think nothing of boarding a plane for a two or three hour flight to the other side of the country. What a blessing!

Lord, I'm grateful for the ability to get from one place to another. You've given man the know-how to develop so many modes of transportation, and I'm thankful for every one! Amen.

83
FRESH CUT GRASS

A fresh-cut yard has an intoxicating smell! It beckons you to come and play, to roll around and toss aside your cares. Just for fun, spend a little time sitting in the grass.

84
ELASTIC WAISTBANDS

Does it sound silly to be thankful for elastic waistbands? If you've eaten too much turkey at Thanksgiving or indulged in a meal with friends, you are likely thankful for that stretchy stuff! God is in the stretching business, too. He's growing us—stretching us—into maturity in our Christian walk.

85

I HAVE A PLACE TO TAKE MY ANXIETIES

We can walk straight into the throne room of the King of Kings and Lord of Lords and lay our troubles at His feet. God is the great burden bearer. He longs for you to cast your cares on Him. Aren't you thankful for a God like that?

Do not be anxious about anything, but in everything, by prayer. . .present your requests to God.

PHILIPPIANS 4:6 NIV

86

THINGS THAT
DIDN'T HAPPEN

How many times have you asked God to make something happen, only to thank Him later that you didn't get what you asked for? Maybe He kept you safe from an accident or a bad relationship situation. We need to thank God not only for the things that happen in our lives, but also for the things that don't!

*I waited patiently for the LORD; he turned to me
and heard my cry. He lifted me out of the slimy pit,
out of the mud and mire; he set my feet on a
rock and gave me a firm place to stand.*

PSALM 40:1–2 NIV

— 87 —
HOT COCOA AND A ROARING FIREPLACE

There's nothing nicer on a cold winter's day than a roaring fire in the fireplace and a mug of hot cocoa on the couch. Talk about the perfect environment for a cozy afternoon!

— 88 —
THE SCENT OF A CHRISTMAS TREE

There's something so intoxicating about the scent of a fresh-cut tree. A Christmas tree causes the imagination to kick in. It takes you back in time to more carefree days. Ah, that beautiful, fragrant tree!

89

MY PROVISIONS

Get specific with the Lord. What provision has He made in your life? A home? A vehicle? A job? A family? Friends? Money to pay the electric bill? Food on the table? Make a list of all of the provisions you're thankful for and put it on your refrigerator so you never forget God's daily goodness to you!

Lord, thank You for providing for me. You've given and given and given again. You make sure my daily needs are met. I don't go without—food, clothing, shelter, or anything else I need. Amen.

90
CHOCOLATE

Ah, what a gift from on high! Chocolate, the soother of the soul. The melt-in-your-mouth remedy for what ails you. Does it seem like a silly thing to be thankful for? It's not! All good gifts come from above. . .and chocolate is one of the best!

91
THE INTERNET

The Internet is a great way to stay in touch with friends, family, and even folks from your school days. God loves it when His kids stay connected!

92

ENCOURAGING PEOPLE

Encouragers lift you up when you're down, bring a smile to your face to replace the frown, and they generally convince you that life will go on, even when it doesn't feel that way. Take time today to thank God for the encouragers in your life, then ask Him to show you how you can be an encouragement to someone else.

Lord, where would I be without the encouragers in my life? They lift my spirits and point me toward You! Thank You for these special people. And please, Father, gift me with encouragement, that I may offer the same hope to others. Amen.

93

COMFORTABLE SHOES

We never think to thank God for comfortable shoes until we're wearing uncomfortable ones! Spend time today thinking about people around the world who don't have shoes to wear. It's strange to think of shoes as a luxury. But that's just what they are!

94

A COMFY COUCH

Whether you're gathered together with family to talk about the happenings of the day, or watching a television show together, there's something so inviting about a cushy, comfy sofa.

95
PEACE

Peace, peace, wonderful peace! Seems nearly impossible in this rush-about world, doesn't it? Close your eyes for a moment and shut out the busyness of the world. Draw in a deep, cleansing breath. Allow God's peace to wash over you like a river. There. . .doesn't that feel great?

Peace I leave with you; my peace I give you.
I do not give to you as the world gives. Do not let
your hearts be troubled and do not be afraid.

JOHN 14:27 NIV

96

A HALF-FULL GLASS

Don't you love people who see the glass as half full? They're so encouraging, so uplifting. What about you? Do you tend to look at life in a more positive light, or do you run on the negative side? Today, pause to think about all of the half-full glasses God has given you over the years, then praise Him for a positive attitude!

Lord, sometimes I need to be reminded
that my glass is half full, not half empty.
May I never forget Your many blessings. Amen.

97
GOOD COOKING

If you're a lover of good food, then you certainly appreciate excellent cooking. Give thanks for the ability to cook well—or for the people in your life who have that gift!

98
MUSIC

Music lifts the spirits when you're down and calms you when you're troubled. And great worship music does even more: It ushers us into the very presence of God. At the touch of a finger—on the radio, Internet, or mp3 player—we can tune in to the song of our choice. What a luxury!

99

FRIENDS WHO STAND
THE TEST OF TIME

True friends are a gift from God. Spend some time thanking Him for the friends who've stood by you through thick and thin. Then commit to be such a friend to those He has placed in your life.

Lord, where would I be without my friends?
You've anointed certain people to walk with me in
the valleys of my life. They've been gifted to hold
my hand when I'm down and laugh with me when
I'm up. Thank You, Father, for these special people.
May I be such a friend to others when they are in need.
Amen.

100
LIMITLESS
POSSIBILITIES

What do you do with all of those possibilities placed in your path? How do you turn them from "what ifs" to realities? Pray about each one. Seek the Lord. Then, as He leads, act. Take that possibility by the horns and watch it become a God-inspired reality.

Delight yourself in the LORD and he will give you the desires of your heart.

PSALM 37:4 NIV

101
GENERATIONS TO COME

Have you ever paused to thank God for the generations that will follow after you? Your children, grandchildren, great-grandchildren, and so forth? If you train up your children in the ways of the Lord, faith can help preserve your family for generations to come. Now, that's something to be thankful for!

102
MANNA FROM HEAVEN

God showers down blessings from heaven, just as He did for the Israelites as they wandered in the desert. He meets our needs—often in unexpected and unusual ways. Next time you're in a barren spot, look up! Might be raining manna from on high!

103

THE EYE OF THE STORM

If you've ever ridden out a storm in a closet or basement, then you know what it's like when the eye passes over. The winds cease and there's a sense of calm—the very center of the storm. Jesus is the eye of life's storms. He's the One—when the winds are swirling around you—to bring peace, comfort, and protection.

So do not fear, for I am with you; do not be dismayed, for I am your God. I will strengthen you and help you; I will uphold you with my righteous right hand.

ISAIAH 41:10 NIV

GOD'S ACCEPTANCE

God doesn't say, "Get cleaned up, kiddo, and then come to Me." No, He looks down at you with every flaw, every sin, every imperfection, and says, "Know what? I adore you!" Talk about feeling loved! Talk about feeling accepted. God's unconditional love toward you is beyond comprehension.

"For the LORD does not see as man sees; for man looks at the outward appearance, but the LORD looks at the heart."

1 SAMUEL 16:7 NKJV

105

THE FREEDOM TO CHOOSE OUR POLITICAL LEADERS

The ability to choose our political leaders through voting is a privilege we often taken for granted. As you pray for our leaders, take the time to thank God for the freedom to choose who will represent you.

106

HOLDING HANDS

Whether you're reaching to clasp the hand of your sweetheart, giving your elderly grandmother's hand a gentle squeeze, or wrapping a toddler's tiny fist with your own, there's something special about holding hands. The next time you reach to take someone's hand, whisper a prayer of thanks for that loved one.

107

THE PRIVILEGE OF ASKING, SEEKING, AND KNOCKING

We serve a God who wants us to ask, seek, and knock. Be thankful He doesn't stand at the door shouting, "Go away! I'm too busy for you!" Instead, He waits for our knock then opens it and ushers us inside, into His presence. What a blessed privilege!

"Everyone who asks receives; he who seeks finds; and to him who knocks, the door will be opened."

MATTHEW 7:8 NIV

108
GOD'S STRENGTH WHEN I AM WEAK

God can prove His strength best when we're at our weakest. Instead of puffing up our muscles and making us look self-sufficient, He allows our weakness to shine through—so that those watching can see He's actually doing the work. Next time you're facing a difficult situation, let God be God. His strong arms can out-muscle yours any day!

God is our refuge and strength,
a very present help in trouble.

PSALM 46:1 KJV

109

PEN, INK, AND PAPER

Whether you love the feel of a pen in your hand or like to type e-mails, it's a blessing to be able to communicate with others. Today, use the gift of writing to pen notes to friends, thanking them for the role they've played in your life.

110

ABUNDANCE TO SHARE

What a privilege it is to share with someone who has a need! Whether it's canned goods given to a food pantry or a gently used jacket to a coat drive, sharing is a blessing to the giver and the receiver.

111

THE PROMISE
OF ETERNAL LIFE

Forever is a mighty long time! We are blessed that we get to spend forever with the One who loves us most, the One who created us, and calls us His own.

I am not ashamed of the gospel of Christ: for it is the power of God unto salvation to every one that believeth.

ROMANS 1:16 KJV

PRAYER

We can communicate with the King of Kings! Praying is so much more than just presenting our wish list to God. It's a great way to stay connected with Him, to tell Him how much we love Him. And our prayer closet is also a great place to lay our troubles down at His feet and seek His will for our lives. Yes, prayer is truly a gift. . .one we should be extremely grateful for.

In every thing by prayer and supplication with
thanksgiving let your requests be made known unto God.

PHILIPPIANS 4:6 KJV

113
KIND PEOPLE

It's so great to come across genuinely kind people. They are usually there to greet you with a smile or a kind word just when you need it. What a blessing! Yes, a little kindness surely goes a long, long way.

114
OUR PLANET

You can see the tip of God's finger carving the Grand Canyon or smell the fragrance of the flowers in the garden. God created planet Earth. . .not only as a place of residence for His children, but as a gift. May it be one we never take for granted!

SONGS IN THE NIGHT

Like the loving Father He is, God sings over us when we face the dark times. He's right there when we're frightened, wrapping His arms around us, reminding us of His eternal presence. Aren't you thankful the Lord walks with you through the dark times? Oh, what an awesome and loving God we serve!

But each day the LORD pours his unfailing love upon me,
and through each night I sing his songs,
praying to God who gives me life.

PSALM 42:8 NLT

116
VISION

The gift of sight is a precious one, indeed. Colors, shapes, scenery, the face of someone you love. . .where would you be if you couldn't see these things? Today, pause to thank the Lord for your sight.

117
GOD'S WONDERS

When you think of the great wonders of the world, what comes to mind? Are they manmade things (the pyramids, the Coliseum, the Great Wall of China) or are they God-made (the Grand Canyon, the Rocky Mountains, Niagara Falls)? God-made wonders win out every time! May we always be thankful for His creative ingenuity!

THOSE WHO HAVE
GONE BEFORE US

Make a list of those people who have paved the way, bringing you to where you are in your spiritual life. Then go through that list, thanking God for each and every one. For the ones who've gone on to be with the Lord, spend some special time reflecting on the special role they played in your life.

Lord, You always know just the right people to send into my life. You've arranged my parents, my Sunday school teachers, and my coworkers. Thank You for those who've gone before me. Amen.

119

JOY

God's supernatural joy is the kind that bubbles up from your midsection and fills you with hope. It gets you through the hard times, giving you a reason to move forward. Best of all, the Lord gives it freely to all who ask. May your joy overflow!

"These things I have spoken to you, that My joy may remain in you, and that your joy may be full."

JOHN 15:11 NKJV

120
COWORKERS

God wants us to realize that we can accomplish more when we work together. So which coworkers are you most thankful for? Take the time to tell God just how grateful you are for every one!

121
THE PATTER OF RAIN
ON A TIN ROOF

Rain on the rooftop gives us an excuse to be still, to stay put. It's an invitation to relax. That's a rare gift these days, and one to be thankful for!

122

THE PARTING OF
THE WATERS

Aren't you thankful for this miracle-working God? How many times has God parted the waters for you? Likely, too many to count!

Father, thank You for parting the waters for me.
I've watched You intervene in my life so many times,
and I'm so grateful for Your many life-changing miracles.
Praise You, Lord! Amen.

123

THE VASTNESS
OF THE OCEAN

The vastness of the ocean represents the greatness and grandeur of God. Compared to us, His creation, God is huge. He's so far beyond what we can imagine, it boggles the mind. Unlike the ocean, the Lord has no beginning and no end. He was and is and is to come.

O Lord God, You have begun to show Your
servant Your greatness and Your mighty hand,
for what god is there in heaven or on earth who can do
anything like Your works and Your mighty deeds?

DEUTERONOMY 3:24 NKJV

124
SUNSETS

We don't want to miss a thing as the bright oranges, reds, and yellows of the setting sun slip over the horizon, giving way to evening shadows. The various shades ignite the imagination and stir our creativity. Ah, the magnificent colors of a sunset!

125
LEFTOVER TURKEY AFTER THANKSGIVING

The turkey—all fifteen to twenty pounds of it—signifies not just God's provision, but also His overwhelming, undeserved abundance. It's more than enough. Plenty for one meal . . .and plenty for days to come. Now, that's something to be thankful for!

126

JESUS, MY BURDEN BEARER

You don't have to carry worries, fears, or sickness alone. Jesus is right there with arms extended, encouraging you to place those things in His strong arms.

Then Jesus said, "Come to me, all of you who are weary and carry heavy burdens, and I will give you rest."

MATTHEW 11:28 NLT

127

MEN AND WOMEN IN THE ARMED SERVICES

As you thank God for your country, spend some additional time thanking Him for those who've offered their lives in service to protect it. Pray for a hedge of protection around them. May they walk under the shadow of the Almighty as they serve.

Father, thank You for those who risk their lives. . .for me. May I never take them for granted. I'm so grateful for these servants and ask You to protect each one. Amen.

128
VACATIONS

What is it about a vacation that we love so much? The opportunity to get away from the job for a few days? Close, intimate time with family? The ability to break out of the mundane and into something adventurous? Perhaps it's all of the above. But one thing is for sure: vacations are the best!

129
MASTERED SKILLS

Think of all the skills you've mastered since childhood—learning to walk and talk, reading a book, playing with others. These were the foundations for bigger skills: driving a car, learning an occupation. Yes, mastered skills are certainly something to be thankful for!

130
WARM TOWELS FROM
THE DRYER

There's a tremendous feeling of satisfaction that comes when you wrap yourself in a towel still warm from the dryer. It's comforting, relaxing, and safe. In the same way, the Lord wraps us in His warm, comforting embrace when we're feeling most vulnerable.

Lord, thank You for the simple things—like a towel still warm from the dryer. As I'm wrapped it its warm embrace, may it remind me that You are holding me close and protecting me during my most vulnerable moments. Amen.

BEAUTIFUL ARTWORK

A beautiful piece of art captures the imagination. It causes you to stop and stare. The beauty of God is much like that piece of art—breathtaking. He captures us with that beauty and holds us breathless. The next time you see a beautiful piece of art, remember the ultimate Creator, the One who, with the tip of His finger, created mountains, valleys, sun, moon, and stars!

And let the beauty of the LORD our God be upon us:
and establish thou the work of our hands upon us;
yea, the work of our hands establish thou it.

PSALM 90:17 KJV

132
NEIGHBORS WHO CARE

If you have a neighbor you can call on in a jam, you're truly blessed. If you don't know your neighbors, reach out to them today. Be the kind of neighbor you want to have!

133
SUNSHINE

A sunny day somehow makes everything seem right with the world. Bright sun can melt stress, make problems seem smaller, and add a spring to your step. Sunshine brings temporary joy to our days. But Jesus, the light of the world, brings everlasting joy to our lives.

134

THINGS I TAKE
FOR GRANTED

If someone asked you to make a list of all the things you take for granted, what would be first on the list? Salvation? Intimacy with God? Your health? Your family? Make a list of the things you've taken for granted in your life. Then go through that list—one thing at a time— offering up praises to the Lord for every one!

Lord, sometimes I forget to thank You for things.
I get swept up in living and forget the Giver of life.
May I never take the everyday things for granted again!
Amen.

135

BOOKS WITH HAPPILY-EVER-AFTER ENDINGS

Happily-ever-after endings remind us of the ultimate happily-ever-after ending, when the Lord sweeps in and lifts us to a place where there are no more tears and no more sorrow. Now that's something to look forward to!

For I know the thoughts that I think toward you, says the LORD, thoughts of peace and not of evil, to give you a future and a hope.

JEREMIAH 29:11 NKJV

136
MISSIONARIES

Missionaries share the gospel so freely. And their willingness to sacrifice—comforts, their homeland, family time—often comes at a great cost. If you've never supported missions in the past, ask God to show you a place where you can help.

137
LIFE'S HARD LESSONS

Do you ever feel like you got your degree at the school of hard knocks? Instead of bemoaning the fact that you've made a few mistakes, take the time to thank God for the lessons He's taught you. . .even if they were acquired the hard way!

138

GOD'S EASY YOKE

God's yoke is easy. His burden is light. He's the one carrying the weight! When you're going through a particularly difficult season, He longs for you to hand over the heavy stuff. He's able to bear what you cannot. Give Him your burdens, your fears, your pain. Trust Him to carry what you cannot. Whew! What a relief!

For my yoke is easy, and my burden is light.

MATTHEW 11:30 KJV

RESTORATION

If you've ever refinished a piece of furniture, you know the joy of watching something battered and bruised spring to new life once again. It's the same when God does a work of restoration in your life. What has He restored lately? Your soul? Your attitude? A relationship? Your finances? Today, take the time to thank a generous and loving God for the restoration process He's done in your life.

He restoreth my soul: he leadeth me in the paths of righteousness for his name's sake.

PSALM 23:3 KJV

140

QUIET DINNER
WITH A FRIEND

Oh, the joy of sitting across the table from someone you love. Catching up. Talking about old times. Eating a great meal. In those moments, all of the chaos fades away. Only friendship remains. Now that's something to be thankful for!

141

GOD FINDS US USABLE

Isn't it amazing to think that the God of the universe finds us usable? He's given us specific gifts and abilities for the purpose of reaching out to others. He could have chosen a thousand other ways to reach the unsaved, but the Lord picked us!

142

A TABLE BIG ENOUGH TO HOLD EVERYONE YOU LOVE

It's so much fun to gather around the table for a meal or a game or just for a good talk. Around the table, everyone is relaxed and comfortable. It's truly one of the greatest places to really connect with others.

Lord, I'm so grateful You've placed people in my life that I can fellowship with. Thank You for the special times when we're gathered around the table with people I love. May I never take those moments for granted. Amen.

143
BEST FRIENDS

Best friends lift your arms when you feel you can't go on. They offer words of encouragement and support when you're down. And they speak truth, even when it's hard to hear. Everything is better when you've got someone at your side.

Lord, thank You so much for my best friends.
I don't know where I'd be without them! Bless them
today, Father, and show me how I can be the
best possible friend to them. Amen.

144

ROMANTIC POSSIBILITIES

Ah, love! You see that attractive stranger from across the room and, voilà! Your eyes meet. Your heart races. Could this be. . .love? Oh, the joy of a romantic possibility!

145

GOD'S PROMISES

Sometimes we can't count on people to follow through with what they say they're going to do. That's not true with God, who always keeps His promises. For Him to do otherwise would mean that He isn't God. Live in confidence of His promises today.

146

A MANSION IN HEAVEN

Think of heaven for a moment. A mansion with your name on it. A round-the-clock praise and worship service with the best singers and musicians ever! Spending eternity with the One who created you and loves you most. It's a promise we cling to and a place we look forward to!

"And God will wipe away every tear from their eyes;
there shall be no more death, nor sorrow, nor crying.
There shall be no more pain, for the former
things have passed away."

REVELATION 21:4 NKJV

147

THE ABILITY TO
LOVE THE UNLOVABLE

When we ask, the Lord gives us the capacity to love. . .even when it's hard. The ability to love the unlovable is something only God can accomplish through us. Aren't you grateful you don't have to "try" to love?

"So in everything, do to others what you would have them do to you, for this sums up the Law and the Prophets."

MATTHEW 7:12 NIV

148
COURAGE

No matter how shy or outgoing you may be, there are times in every life that require a heaven-sent jolt of courage. When those times come and God supplies you with the fearlessness you need, be sure to give Him the glory.

149
LEISURE TIME

Though they may be rare, a few hours with nothing to do are a blessing straight from God. Kick back, relax, spend time reconnecting with family or friends—rest in the Father.

150
BOUNDARIES

Boundaries are like a fence around a yard. They keep the bad guys out and give us a clear perspective of where we belong. They hint of safety. Think of the boundaries God has placed in your life. Aren't you grateful for every one?

You have done many good things for me, LORD,
just as you promised. I believe in your commands;
now teach me good judgment and knowledge.

PSALM 119:65—66 NLT

151
BIRDS OUTSIDE MY WINDOW

Have you ever watched a bird through your window? Observed his brilliant colors? Pondered the way he flits so easily from the branch of a tree to the windowsill? Listened to his lighthearted song? There's something so magnificent about watching this tiny creature fly from place to place, isn't there? And what a great reminder. . .he's free to go where he feels led without fear. He's also confident enough in himself to allow a watching world observe him as he does so. A lesson for us, perhaps?

Thank You, Lord, for the reminder that I can soar as freely as that bird outside my window, as long as I'm listening to Your still, small voice. Amen.

152
RIGHT CHOICES

We're faced with choices at every turn. Sure, we occasionally falter and make the wrong choice, but think of all of the right ones you've made with God's help throughout the years!

153
CLEANSING TEARS

Tears are cleansing. They are a release of anxiety, fears, emotional hurts, and even physical pain. If we had no tears, where would the pain go? Earthly tears are a necessity, but praise God. . .there's coming a day in heaven when we won't need them anymore!

RIGHTEOUS LEADERSHIP

Thank God for righteous leaders—presidents, senators, mayors, pastors, parents. They bring honor to the Lord with their godly examples. Take time to list the many righteous leaders He has placed in your life. Then spend time lifting each person up in prayer. And while you're doing that, rededicate yourself to righteousness.

Lord, with so much wickedness in this world,
I'm amazed by those righteous ones who stand firm,
like trees by the water. Guard the leaders in my life,
Father, and help me to be a righteous leader as well.
Amen.

LIFE, LIBERTY, AND THE PURSUIT OF HAPPINESS

Pause to thank your heavenly Father for each of these things. Life: what a precious gift! Liberty: our very freedom. The pursuit of happiness: we're free to pursue our lives in Christ without fear or bondage. Aren't you grateful for these three precious gifts?

For you have been called to live in freedom,
my brothers and sisters. But don't use your freedom
to satisfy your sinful nature. Instead, use your
freedom to serve one another in love.

GALATIANS 5:13 NLT

156
A NEW DAY

Each new morning is a reminder of God's faithfulness. When you first awaken, before you ever lift your head from the pillow, pause to thank the Lord for another day. Then make a commitment to walk in thankfulness, grateful for each minute.

157
DAYS THE BATHROOM SCALE STAYS EVEN

If you're someone who struggles with weight issues, perhaps you approach the scale nervously, wondering what the number will be today. If so, be thankful for the days when the number stays the same—or even goes down!

158
CELEBRATIONS

O h, how we wait for the special days on the calendar to arrive! Whether it's a birthday, a holiday, or a celebration of an achievement, these times allow us to reconnect with friends and family in a special way. Find something new to celebrate today!

"You will go out in joy and be led forth in peace;
the mountains and hills will burst into song before you,
and all the trees of the field will clap their hands."

ISAIAH 55:12 NIV

159
TIME, THE GREAT HEALER

God is our healer. But did you ever consider the role time plays in the healing process? Time mends broken hearts. It gives us a chance for pain to lessen and for wounds to close. Aren't you thankful when you are given the time to fully mend?

Father, I recognize that much of my healing—
emotional, physical, and otherwise—has come about
in Your timing, not my own. Thank You so
much for giving me the gift of time. Amen.

160
AN EVER-PRESENT GOD

Does it boggle your mind to know that the Creator of the universe is only a heartbeat away? When you call. . .He answers. Praise the Lord! He's only a prayer away!

161
EXERCISE

Ah, exercise! It lifts us from our hum-drum state, gets our blood pumping, and strengthens us, inside and out. Whether you're making the rounds at the gym, riding your bike, or jogging in the park, take the time to thank God for the gift of exercise. It's a gift He hopes you'll use. . .often!

162
UMBRELLAS

An umbrella protects you from the elements, keeping your clothes dry and your hairdo intact. In a similar way, God covers us with His love, His blessings, and His provision. He shields us from life's many storms.

I am overwhelmed with joy in the LORD my God! For he has dressed me with the clothing of salvation and draped me in a robe of righteousness. I am like a bridegroom in his wedding suit or a bride with her jewels.

ISAIAH 61:10 NLT

163

COMFORT FOR THOSE
WHO MOURN

The Spirit of God is your comforter, a very present help when you're in trouble. He blankets you and gives peace. He can—and will—turn your mourning into dancing. . .if you let Him.

Lord, only You can bring comfort for those who mourn.
Entertainment can't do it. A cheerful word from a friend
can't do it. Truly, the only comfort I can find when I've
been at the bottom of the well is the overpowering,
all-encompassing arms of my heavenly Father. Amen.

164
GOOD ADVICE

Wise words from a close friend or family member are like hearing a beautiful melody. After going to the Father in prayer, there is no better way to get good advice than asking for help from someone you trust.

165
FUNNY TV SHOWS

Don't you love funny television shows? The characters captivate us with their wit, and the ridiculous plotlines make us laugh. What is it about humor that gets to us, anyway? Perhaps it's the fact that we really love to laugh at ourselves. In those television characters, we catch a glimpse. . .of us!

SILLY MOMENTS

Silly moments catch us by surprise and bring laughter, usually when we need it most! Giving yourself the freedom to be silly is not just okay, it's actually good for you. After all, laughter is great medicine. And in this hectic world we live in, we can use a few silly moments!

So I recommend having fun, because there is nothing better for people in this world than to eat, drink, and enjoy life. That way they will experience some happiness along with all the hard work God gives them under the sun.

ECCLESIASTES 8:15 NLT

167
BABY'S FIRST STEPS

O h, the joy of watching that little darling teeter this way and that on unsteady feet. Don't you imagine God feels the same way when He looks down on us, His kids? We falter at times, but what joy we must bring to His heart when our steps are steady and sure.

He has showed you, O man, what is good. And what does the LORD require of you? To act justly and to love mercy and to walk humbly with your God.

MICAH 6:8 NIV

168

THE INNOCENCE
OF TINY CHILDREN

Little children bring such joy to the heart! They're so innocent, so sweet. They're a true reflection of God's goodness, through and through.

169

THE GREAT OUTDOORS

It's great to find a spot away from the crowd, a place where the beauty of nature captivates you. Aren't you thankful for these wonderful reminders that life can be found outside the four walls of your home or office?

A PERSONAL RELATIONSHIP WITH THE KING OF KINGS

Picture yourself walking into the throne room of God Almighty. No need to fear this King! He's been waiting on you. He wants to wrap you in His arms and tell you just how special you are to Him.

Lord, thank You for the private invitation into Your throne room. I'm so grateful to be welcomed as Your child! Amen.

171

EMOTIONAL HEALING

What emotional sickness are you dealing with today? Whatever pain, anguish, or sorrow you're holding onto, may this be the day you hand it off to the ultimate Physician, the One who can wipe away every tear and make you completely whole.

*He heals the brokenhearted and binds up their wounds.
. . . Great is our Lord, and mighty in power.*

PSALM 147:3, 5 NIV

172
HOPE

A life without hope is like a tire without air. When our hope fizzles away, we slip into an attitude of defeat. God longs to infuse us with supernatural hope, not just to brighten our day, but to confirm His love and care in our lives.

So be strong and courageous,
all you who put your hope in the LORD!

PSALM 31:24 NLT

173
CELEBRATIONS

Everyone loves a great party. . .and there are so many opportunities to celebrate! God loves for us to share life's victories together. The next time you're in the mood for a party, invite your brothers and sisters in the Lord. . .and make sure God is in the center of it!

174
POLITE DRIVERS

Some people are so hurried that they often take out their frustrations behind the wheel. That's why it's so refreshing to find a polite driver—someone who yields the right of way. Decide to not only appreciate polite drivers. . . but to be one!

— 175 —
JOY IN THE MORNING

Have you ever gone to bed completely over-whelmed? Then, wonder of wonders! You awoke to a brand-new day! Maybe the problems weren't gone, but the despair was! The sun through the window and the dew on the grass made you hope again and restored your joy.

For His anger is but for a moment,
His favor is for life; weeping may endure
for a night, but joy comes in the morning.

PSALM 30:5 NKJV

BROTHERS AND SISTERS IN CHRIST

If you're a Christian, you belong to the biggest family ever. And our Daddy God is the ultimate Father. Make a list of all of the Christian brothers and sisters who've had an impact on your life over the past few months, then thank God for every one!

"For where two or three come together in my name, there am I with them."

MATTHEW 18:20 NIV

177
MEMORIES

The Creator God has blessed us humans with the ability to remember and reflect on happy times in our past. These special memories that we share with family and friends strengthen our relationships now and for the future.

178
PERSEVERANCE

As you go through seasons of perseverance, hold tight to God's promises. Continue to praise Him. Those who are watching will learn a lot by seeing how you handle this season!

179

EMPOWERMENT TO PROCLAIM GOOD NEWS!

Never underestimate the power of your own story to open doors and change lives. Aren't you grateful the Lord can use what you've been through—good and bad—to touch others?

"The Spirit of the Lord is on me, because he has anointed me to preach good news to the poor. He has sent me to proclaim freedom for the prisoners and recovery of sight for the blind, to release the oppressed."

LUKE 4:18 NIV

180
DIVINE INTERVENTION

If you've ever almost been in an accident, then you know the relief of a near miss! Maybe you've had a few other near misses, as well: a job you almost accepted; a wedding that almost moved forward; a temptation you managed to resist. Sometimes those near misses are divine intervention from God.

Father, I'm so grateful that You've protected me from harm, not just in the physical sense (my body) but my heart, mind, and emotions, as well. I'm so grateful for Your divine intervention! Amen.

181
INFECTIOUS GIGGLES

Nothing excites the heart like giggles between friends and family. Join in as laughter erupts. You will feel like a kid again when you celebrate life's little joys!

182
A BRIDE'S SMILE

A bride's smile radiates joy as she walks down the aisle toward her husband-to-be. Moments like that are meant to be cherished—when all of the cares of life fade away and only anticipation of good things remain.

183
I HAVE AN ADVOCATE

An advocate is someone who runs interference for you. He defends you when you cannot defend yourself and plays the role of mediator, speaking on your behalf. Jesus Christ is the ultimate Advocate. He chose to run interference for us when He gave His life on the cross. Best of all, He paid the price.

"But the Counselor, the Holy Spirit, whom the Father will send in my name, will teach you all things and will remind you of everything I have said to you."

JOHN 14:26 NIV

BIBLE HEROES

Aren't you grateful for the story of young David, who took down the mighty giant, Goliath? Does the story of Joshua marching around the walls of Jericho give you hope? The story of Shadrach, Meshach, and Abednego in the fiery furnace challenges us to stand firm in our faith till the end. Praise the Lord for such great biblical examples.

Lord, I want to have the courage of Daniel, the patience of Joshua, the tenacity of Shadrach, Meshach, and Abednego. I want to do great and mighty things for You. Thank You for these examples. They give me such hope! Amen.

MENTORS AND MENTEES

God sends people into your circle who can share their expertise with you. What a blessing! And it's wonderful to know that you have something of value to share with others. Mentoring is truly one of the best ways to give of yourself.

Lord, I'm so grateful for the many mentors You've sent my way. I've learned so much from them and my cup is so full! May I take what I've learned and share it with others You place in my circle of influence. Amen.

186

A CLEAN HOUSE

Oh, the joy of a clean house! Not just "sort of" clean but really, truly clean, from top to bottom. No dust. No dirty dishes. No unmade beds. No laundry to do. There's nothing like it!

Create in me a clean heart, O God;
and renew a right spirit within me.

PSALM 51:10 KJV

TREKS THROUGH
THE DESERT

Have you ever spent a season of your life in the desert? Maybe, like the Israelites, you've wandered around and around in circles, going nowhere. Instead of bemoaning the fact that you've spent time in the desert, thank God for those dry seasons. Those times prepare you to appreciate the beauty of the Promised Land.

Behold, I will do a new thing; now it shall spring forth; shall ye not know it? I will even make a way in the wilderness, and rivers in the desert.

ISAIAH 43:19 KJV

188
GOD'S MERCY

When God extends His hand of mercy, He's really offering you compassion, kindness, forgiveness, and understanding. God isn't standing over you, waiting for you to fail. No, we serve a merciful God, full of grace and love for His kids.

I will sing of the mercies of the LORD for ever: with my mouth will I make known thy faithfulness to all generations.

PSALM 89:1 KJV

FRIENDS AND LOVED ONES
I HAVE YET TO MEET

Have you ever thought about the friends and loved ones you haven't even met yet? Who will they be? What impact will they have on your life? The Lord brings people together in the most wonderful ways—at church, at work, in neighborhoods, in families.

*Lord, it's exciting to think of the people I will be
close to in the future. I don't know them yet,
but one day we'll be the best of friends.
Thank You for the friends I have now. . .
and the ones I have yet to meet. Amen.*

190

THE SPARKLE IN
A SPOUSE'S EYES

Married couples seem to have a secret language all their own, a code of sorts. They can discern expressions and gauge moods at a glance. Best of all, they can read joy and mirth in the other person's face before a word is spoken. How wonderful to have a spouse who knows you that well!

A present is a precious stone in the eyes of its possessor;
wherever he turns, he prospers.

PROVERBS 17:8 NKJV

191

PHYSICAL HEALING

Think about all of the times you've battled a cold or flu. Aren't you glad those sicknesses didn't go on forever? The Great Physician brings us relief and miraculous healing—even in the routine illnesses.

Lord, I thank You for the many times You've healed me physically. You've been so good to make me strong again. May I never forget that You are my healer. By Your stripes, I am healed. Amen.

192
CONTENTMENT

To find contentment in your current situation is truly a gift from God. The world tells us to want more and more, but God tells us to sit back and appreciate the many blessings He has already given. Ask Him, and He'll show you how to be content in any situation.

But godliness with contentment is great gain.

1 TIMOTHY 6:6 NIV

AN EXCELLENT HARVEST

After the prep work, the planting, the nurturing, the watering, and the pruning, a better-than-expected result is a wonderful blessing because of a season of hard work. God rewards our diligence in harvests of all kinds.

Let us not become weary in doing good, for at the proper time we will reap a harvest if we do not give up.

GALATIANS 6:9 NIV

194
GOD-ANSWERS

God's answers to our questions (Where should I work? What school should I go to? Who should I marry? Where should I live?) are always the best choice. The next time you're facing a big decision, look first to God for answers. It will save you so much time and trouble! Aren't you grateful that the Lord has everything all figured out?

Trust in the LORD with all your heart and lean not on your own understanding; in all your ways acknowledge him, and he will make your paths straight.

PROVERBS 3:5–6 NIV

SCRIPTURE THAT COMES TO MIND IN TIMES OF NEED

Maybe you're feeling alone and "Lo, I am with you" comes to mind. Perhaps you're scared and suddenly you're reminded. . . "I have not given you a spirit of fear, but of power, love, and a sound mind." There's a Bible verse for every situation. God uses His Word to remind you that He's got you covered.

How precious to me are your thoughts, O God!
How vast is the sum of them! Were I to count them,
they would outnumber the grains of sand.

PSALM 139:17–18 NIV

196

THE FIRST FLOWER
IN SPRING

The wintertime can be long and a little dreary. Oh, but that first sign of spring! The day you discover buds on the trees or a blooming flower. It causes you to hope, to think ahead, to see the possibilities. What a joyous gift!

The flowers appear on the earth;
the time of the singing of birds is come,
and the voice of the turtle is heard in our land.

SONG OF SOLOMON 2:12 KJV

197
GOD'S MAJESTY

The majesty of Almighty God far surpasses that of any earthly king. He dazzles us with His splendor, amazes us with His great beauty. He rules, not with an iron fist, but out of overwhelming love. His majesty and power are seen, not in robes and crowns, but in the great beauty of His presence and in His heart for His children.

O LORD, our Lord,
how majestic is your name in all the earth!

PSALM 8:9 NIV

198

BIRTH AND REBIRTH

The birth experience is so miraculous, so unexplainable. God designed it to be a great mystery. Being born again into the family of God is equally as miraculous and mysterious. Thank Him today for allowing you to be born—twice!

"Where, O death, is your victory? Where, O death, is your sting?" The sting of death is sin, and the power of sin is the law. But thanks be to God! He gives us the victory through our Lord Jesus Christ."

1 CORINTHIANS 15:55—57 NIV

I'M NOT IN CHARGE!

The minute you let go of the control you have in your life, the minute you acknowledge that God alone is in charge, the sooner He's able to move on your behalf. You were never meant to handle this on your own, anyway. He knows best how—and when—to intervene in the lives of His children.

Then Jesus came to them and said, "All authority in heaven and on earth has been given to me."

MATTHEW 28:18 NIV

STRENGTHEN YOUR PRAYER LIFE
WITH THIS GREAT SERIES FROM
BARBOUR PUBLISHING:

Power Prayers for Women
978-1-59789-670-2

Power Prayers for Men
978-1-59789-858-4

Power Prayers to Start Your Day
978-1-59789-859-1

Power Prayers for Your Marriage
978-1-60290-460-5

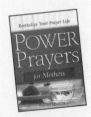

Power Prayers for Mothers
978-1-59789-998-7

Available wherever books are sold.